T0308020

EAVESdrop

EAVESdrop

poems & drawings

overhearing others

SARAH RIGGS

chax
2020

Copyright ©2020 by Sarah Riggs. All rights reserved.

ISBN 978-1-946104-23-6

Library of Congress Control Number: 2020932551

chax press / 1517 n wilmot rd / tucson arizona 85712-4410

Chax Press books are supported in part by individual donors and by sales of the books. Please visit *https://chax.org/membership-support/* if you would like to contribute to our mission to make an impact on the literature and culture of our time.

Cover image used with permission from the artist.
Yto Barrada, *Indiscret*, 2018, model for a conversation chair.

Author Acknowledgments:
Deep thanks to the many writers and artists and friends and family who have helped generate this work, and specifically to the following spaces and journals: *Belladonna Collaborative, Brooklyn Arts Exchange, The Capilano Review, Chergui, Contrat Maint, Litmus Press,* and *The Poetry Project.*

CONTENTS

for my mother
and daughters
and all beings

(from Davi Kopenawa, "another sky")

THE SKY

Our elders did not have image skins and did not write laws on them. Their only words were those pronounced by their mouths and they did not draw them. So their words never went far away from them and this is why the white people have never known them.

Davi Kopenawa, *The Falling Sky*

Written for a collaboration with Omar Berrada for the Sursock Museum, Beirut

Elements of a World: The Sky

the sky

falls furiously and softly

a window with a ledge with eyes looking through it

a shield with holes in it

a source

a receptacle

wandered off again

does not make exceptions

renders us nothing

witnesses the diminishing population of sea turtles

thoroughly cloudy

full of drones

collected into itself

an impact of emissions

a collection

13

mildly ambitious

knows each street from above and below

a series of admissions

doesn't know everything

a biography of Rabi'à al'Adawiyya

not hurtful

not the sum of its parts

has a problem

waits for the forest

cannot be cured by doctors

deepens at your thought

a weight

inarticulate

articulate mass of cultures and forms

in itself

a splintered holster of ideas

regrettably small when you look at it this way

bouncing with ideas

huge with itself and more than itself

has held up all this time

a tempered mass of stars

is threaded matter

a string we are pulling

going up

has a tail

a temper

going down

half-way down

three-quarters down

the sky is a blur

falls furiously softly still

says hello

good-bye

reverses

a shield with holes in it

a source

a receptacle

is drizzling

not hurtful

does not make exceptions

a place

not the sum of its parts

has a problem

cannot be cured by doctors

a weight

in itself

a splintered holster of ideas

regrettably small when you look at it this way

bouncing with ideas

huge with itself and more than itself

deepens at your thought

knows about these lines

knows you are overhearing

has held up all this time

Note 1 on "eavesdrop": listening to internal thoughts is somewhat like listening to other speech not addressed to you, but what you overhear. There is a navigation there not just between outside and inside, but between the outside of the outside, and the inside of the inside— there are then at least four layers of speech in any waking experience. It is overwhelming to think about, to perceive, to take in, which is why it is sometimes relaxing to sleep and enter the cacophony of dream language. Each sequence tries differently to balance languages, bringing the ear in touch with the whole of thinking bodies, and the drawings work at drawing out the body of reading, of slowing down words, so that they reach into the space around them and through us, porously.

OR — HEARD (crisis)

The vertical interior of the Americas
dreamt my spine, pulling through the eye
of each vertebra a tactile thread

> —Liz Howard, *Infinite Citizen of the Shaking Tent*

The world is in the book,
in your eyes, the rising
death toll

> —Maged Zaher, *Words from Bent Bones*

Your brain is always eavesdropping on your thoughts. As it listens,
it leans. If you teach it about limitation, your brain will become
limited . . .

> —Deepak Chopra

(from Gail Scott, "Things were NOT Going well")

So they quipped and bickered and bit
it was like them, to bring the stars
underfoot and render the time a point
of contention rather than a beautiful
mingling of constantly translating spaces

We wished for our friends, the
circle of them, or pastry parallelogram,
only in this way, laying into the
fire, troubled or indecent, terribly our,
sickly, diseased, tremendously vulgar, in power

The flesh of the hour was red, was yellow,
was black, is red, is yellow, is black
to have to reach to the bone to
feel what we have in common—red,
yellow, black no puns, nor play, colors.

The horrendous charge of humanity
and one wished for Zeus to pull on the reigns
or back again to that hour, tripping
over the wires under the ocean—there is
a wire quand même listening in there

If it was never for the hour
so ruthlessly prolonged, chirping there
in a sullen seat, politically electrically
charged: shapen this way and that
(hollow to the moon, you say you say)

What they wired in that space so there
a reckless freedom in the containment
gender and gender, race and gender,
all of race and race, swimming so
many dolphins (intelligent) in a sharked sea

Tore from them, making a space, making
spaces, if not for that, the serious
vote, being one point amid a tangle a
cluster a terrorized mass, and then
blinking, holding back and onto that thing

Reminds me of E, constantly making,
that place in the middle of a broach
which knows its needle, a woman in
power, just one, no not even, never
even, slipping down to a penisless space

Quand même je voulais que tu écoutes
ton maître, maître d'E, pas pour
longtemps, mais quand-même, dans le
sacrifice de la mélancolie, les plaisirs
du langage abound (même si c'est ça)

23

Frustrating to encounter a hole in an
ought, when it's really a sieve, and
J there smoking a cigarette all over
Brooklyn (not maimed, downtrodden yes, but
tending tenderly to the tinkering of the second)

The Rorsarch test (I can't even spell it)
rocking on the balance of bedtime and life:
It was kind of precarious, the remainder
Of that hour, it's like these words:
Hour, second, remainder→her mountain

Theirs, theirs, she was forgetting again
and letting it sway to the side (I'm not
used to it). Night and pointing and
U girl (that was it). The freedoms
crashing together into one giant globe-wreck

Tearing at their hair, pulling at it,
by the braids, and the seams between
braids, on the scalps, in that place
carnivorous and deeply troubling.
(translated to the emergency room, said T)

How to market it, to make it, to
endure the twisting of the response into
a high end word slap. Paw upon paw
torn at the power of the weight shift.
A million women walking together out of step.

As if it were happening over there,
somewhere far away, knee deep in
water, the sickening reality of that,
however it was organized, the
grim determinant of the lesser known

Removal. And its fact so venomous
that removal of grievances was not
possible. Graves could not be dug
up and planted with clean soil, clean
earth. The world was sobbing (Is, will be)

Such the lick of time, into the textured
east, and a thousand veils falling over
a million women (not enough, not enough)
The collective scream not enough because
the screaming was at each other

A tender reserve of screams collected
in jars and presented in white galleries
and the hullabaloo of the fierce
peoples, the masks, the dresses on heads,
such material is fascinating for research

It was a wallop of fine rain
and they wintered in illusions and
polluted pelicans but the love was
there (witness) such cantankerous
postcards and fine writing instruments sent through the eye

Meanwhile writing and rewriting to A in prison
but could not summon the strength to send
the knowledge of not knowing the
conditions, horrifying that lack of power—
to infuse with love. Saudi Arabia here in my ear's eye

There was the certainty T that
You are not in a safe space on the
subway, on the street, on the
telephone, anywhere even with your friends
your family even with (I am sorry)

Taking the temperature of the times,
it comes out sub-degree zero
and yet the connections are very strong,
very warm very trustworthy, worthy, thy
tie, in a y, or a t-shape, oh

Fermently caughtious or arraigned
the words M on your slip of an
eye which is really a paw (such is
laughter & the immensity by which
I meant that) so and so and so

On to something else, the alarm
goes off, the snooze is not infinite,
there are things to be awake to
query there and foreground the honest
(it is a zone) such that this

The remainder of what you had to say
there in the béchamel sauce in the
voting booth (so pointless if important)
they were looking at you or to you
just briefly for a second but it mattered

At that time she did ten paintings with lines
in black and purple (the sadness gaping
from the wounds) very straight
though not continuous, the lines telling
nothing telling in a particular way

Dear M, in a meander, the threads
tangled, and you there free glimpsed in a sauna
how could it be otherwise, the smile,
and the thoughtfulness, everything vegan
the fists love and hate, and then yours, open

I heard what it was you meant, though not said
there were branches growing out of her head
and at this point, no leaves, but berries
and the occasional black squirrel pondering
there, and you asked, "how do I fly?"

Other than these memories, the present could
not contain us, and we were flying back
back, looking at the trauma dug into the
ground, looking at pictures of piles of
bodies (J wrote they were in the river)

Or there was a flow, and these notes
pittering in, an array of voices, some
violence, and they were at Standing Rock
(you vote with your feet) Another J
for instance was there (thank you for this)

Now there were facts (a flow of extremist
cabinet ministers) she could not pick
up that paper, even one piece of it,
without a large boulder weighing impossibly
there (and J was cutting the pieces)

If we could re-glue them together
there would be a treatise of whoever
was gluing, and that is all. Some glue,
and a subjectivity, carrying nations,
cultural belongings, not being able to untear

The flow came easily to them, bitten
out of boulders, the chewable kind
wand, it was like that, hard, like
chewing on your own knuckles,
and there was blood, really, but elsewhere

What she was saying sort of made
sense, that's what it was like,
an in and an out of a sort of,
the surest thing was to go to Vancouver
and to be charged and humbled

If it could be said if it could be written
all that thickness of research
flapped into a fold or nearly, under
that understood: all the women and
girls were saying it marching along together

Feeling along some sort of thread, a spiderwoman
of sorts, and then scrabbling back up the wing
wishing to rejoin the gutter, back and back,
Intzy intzy, wish wash up frame
no surrender, rain and sun, in a loop, crawling

Toppling into tea, a sort of 6-foot dormouse
greeting you nonsensically, though this
having the most of love, the craziness of
saying the crazy, Ethan the faun
inviting you to tea (and his house, torn)

If your friends were to freeze mid-step
their teeth bared, there wasn't time
to pet their cool metal backs, you had
to go toward the frozen heart of things
(yes the word war is appropriate)

And not wrench it out, somehow
Love would have to win but the ending
of the story not known, and melting
ice apparently not the right metaphor
& what if there were not heart at the core

33

Rewriting histories very very quickly
to achieve a different ending
(such was not in the future but present
now and at this second for instance)
That's what G was saying about love

We could have heard but for
our ears, covered in a sort of
political sauce, to be written by
distant peoples also motivated
by some basic needs (we had forgotten to ask)

Sorry, and the word not remotely enough.
Apology. Not remotely enough.
Remotely. That was the thing.
We had forgotten again. The western world
everywhere, in remote streams, the tongues of frogs

34

Taught at the rim of the last sought edges
into a meager determinant of beauty
wildlife caught in the mesh of goodness
(to preserve) and the words displanted
because of the rage of dreams

And this is nothing new, has been true
all along. The trick to terrorism
how it grows out of anger, and it is
that anger needing to be addressed,
not the terrorism. Not told slant

The slope of the slant very strong now
and a feeling of catapulting collectively
and being next to people very opposite
and yet not because very human
yet the mood very angry and so

35

The wind through the wind of it
Earth you could not touch, violence
you did not have to endure: the way
power enters the psyche and tries to
take control (the victories, victories)

And if she was held back, could they still
be friends, the woman with the beautiful
scarves, one wrapped around her head, asked
and then to clarify, explained that if
she were held back, could we still be friends

Poignant and remarked, fistfuls of rampant
lines, it was you, and it was you, down there
in a rushing, the bodies and the bones
(just words there in the schoolbooks)
How were we to mind the gap?

Etel and Babia, alive at the moment of words,
hovering in the love that inflects their
bodies, words connected to body, and we
a constellation, held in the night, even after
as the conniving ministers appointed day by day

Objects embued with a who-ness
among them a sea otter, a raven-eagle,
a wolf, a whale. The supernatural
helpers so needed "everything must change"
Already one—the better of evils (drones)

Even in the rain, they were, and how
the inversion sudden and strong, who
the giant pandas waiting there, wallowing
in an air infused with rainbows and pollution
a thing in this place, to the hour

37

A tossed vote (wasn't sure who) and the
consequences oily, weighted by genocide
some victories, in North Carolina and
North Dakota, protesting helping,
necessary, and then torn, into that

The past of a paw, into that honey
a trap or an infused bill
frozen and dethawing the articles
of faith, who had heard of tie
sketched that skin so as to break

How to remainder, the cars flitting,
the planes one after another, edging
off experience, the whiteness, what
wash and tame zone, can we just
drop that word white now and let it go

Somewhere in the annals, more or less
held there, a sense of explosion
and capture, it was not possible
to render otherwise: the doors in—
the doors would have to open and let go

(for some poets from Vancouver)

(from Charles Reznikoff, "holding a piece of plank before his face")

TRANSLATIONS FROM DANCE
while writing dance and dancing writing
at the Brooklyn Arts Exchange

To translate a text is to enter into the most intimate relationship with it possible. It is the translator's body, almost more than the translator's mind, that is the vessel of transfer. The mind equates words, expressions, deals with techniques and logistics; it is within the body that the real alchemy— mysterious, unnamed and inexplicable— takes place.

—Lina Mounzer, "War in Translation: Giving Voice to the Women of Syria" (*Literary Hub*)

...de dégager encore mieux l'enjeu véritable de l'art — non pas renvoyer à un sens (intelligible), mais produire du sens ni sensible ni intelligible, en un sens qui se dérobe à cette différence — et, de manière plus précise, de dégaer l'enjeu de la danse.

to extract even further the true stakes of the art—not to refer to a meaning (intelligible) but to produce meaning neither perceptible nor intelligible, in a meaning that evades this difference—and, in a more precise manner, to release the stakes of dance.

—Jean-Luc Nancy with Mathilde Monnier, *Allitérations, Conversations sur la danse*

Quickened on the leg so permanent excellent
We have banished the word "perfect" from dancing here
And so told the exercises to the left hedonistically
It was for you and for you the half of it
Language through a sieve or heightened container so
The leg, don't forget the leg, the other one (of three)
You side-saddle the questions figure it so side-saddled
Step, step, step and again (the language of flowers)
Body and soul conversed, traversed, there crossed
Couldn't keep count: a woman was dancing Maya

Dance flowers in a permanent exchange hollow
Mystified by the columnular setting queer queer
Is good and L walked along that line
There was never just one, never even a line

The topical reminder to be & to write about dance
Free, free the movers cross the ground (floor stage)
Throw into gesture back and forward are not simple
Out of element finding what one can do
She flew back and forth to encounter the contours
of her body. Sink, avenue and horse. Skin
into this bag of rejections a sort of truth hung
Quick, bark, fellow and happened, yellow matter
Pull, pull, to the left, in syncopation, together
They were fleeting, ringing, to the right
Coming around into some sort of middle position
What was back there circling around (age age)
Until one couldn't forget, the slow rising body
That which they sidestepped markedly hollow

(what they wanted to say about the body
was not to forget it, abuse it, or judge it. A
kind of listening in order to tame the abuses.)
Such was what I was thinking at the time,
maybe. (It was this: the thinking was doing
a kind of dance and for the body to be in synch
with that rather than resisting or being bashed
around.) There wasn't a feeling of freedom of
moving outside what the body or thought could
do, rather that the two could "move" together

create a feeling of freedom, which is to say, self-
knowing. They are giving this brain body
"the movement of thought"—the physical
manifestations of wild thinking

a form in the freedom of the kind: orange
and a ration in the stupor of momentum: Clarinda
a forthcoming resolution of how: tapered
and a terrible removal of speed: vanity
a quickening pick of sloth: team
and a formidable shunning of nothing: brazen
a quirky removal of hands: none
and a bottle of liquid dreams: ferment
a solid reminder of feet: sky
and a rationless giving at sun: night
a technical removal of thought: body
and a forcible conditioning of ice: sliding
a thicker container of words: fingers
and a breaching of the mind-body dilemma: improv

a thorough narrows through the cracks: feet
assembly of people and syllables: tenuous
frozen hallway of temperate cacti: thorns
suggestive tint of alley: deciduous

into and out of frequently demanding: fingerprint
forgotten shuttle thick wayward: stamp
the bifurcated trickery of lens: Nebraska
well-meaning divisions of languages: polyglot

tremendous inculcations of dough: putrefaction
foreign and traded submissions: elbow
torn meals and homeless signs: articulate
forever training the summer lids: closure

melting and assuming late tendencies: love
the hollow and rendered clothes: scarecrow
a talented quickening at the lens: ankles
under the qualitative formidable: q-tips

where figurine hours and tickets: shaven
drop to school and rotation blankly: crossed T's
throat melting and surrendering: economy
how virulent and costly the sky: plastic

wished booklets and some teeth: traffic
fortunately applicable the swaying: highways
lifts and dumb bells frought with politics: no
queenly coffees and tapas: she is coming

forgiveness to the drop and drip: terrific
or humble either way voting: formidable
costly in the byways her determination: yes
tinkling possibility of connectivity: on

the way of things, there in that shaft: split
hollow and knee, eyelash, falling away: thorough
foaming and colloquial, last impressions: it
tossed about in universes, one last one: planet

thoroughly removed from that canon: torrential
harvested and kindly, a referendum: drachma
lastly surrendered and remarkable: starlight
the worsted individual, swinging in that: tree

fermenting in the hearing of it: ear strangeness
the crosswords rocked in an embrace: next door
quickly the fox sand shore and now this: street
arms definitely roaming, she asked her: archivist
and a revolutionary stir, coming under the door: Lispector
under and next to and around, released: moment

for Aya Nabih

Note 2 on "eavesdrop": In this work, there are many versions of eavesdropping—which includes incessant citation, which is what happens when I really love a piece of writing. It is like it penetrates my internal language sphere, but there is still a negotiation, and a sense of surprise, as the depths of my brain encounter difference, and this language that is not mine but that I love so much starts to inhabit the language that comes out.

RABI'À JOURNAL

Rabi'à al-'Adawiyya was born and lived in Basra, 717 A.D. through 801, a woman, poet and saint, identified with the Sufis.

"When I thought I saw beneath the skin of the text, and wrote what I saw."

> — Charles Upton, on translating "versions" of Rabi'à al-'Adawiyya in *Doorkeeper of the Heart* (Pir Press, 1988), quoted here in italics with some variations.

(from Rabi'à al-Àdawiyya, "first the neighbor then the house")

Blend I

It was in your hair   She wore
Down her back   *like separation*   torn between
Influence   *out of one second*   on silent meditations
the meeting time opens   the last of the thyme   *the truth*
He isn't outside it   (*I don't want the House inside*)
Rabi'à how do you see?
now flipped over, we had heard all that before
listening in some rooms   *the hours I spend with you*
scattered here and there   *the substance of my complaint*
mostly things were slow to change
Or else the change was not good   *a stranger in your country*
Toni said the extreme far right
without seeing your face?   is coming for us

Blend II

The cupolas added later
And the mix of everything to rest
Cup, wine, and friend make three
Housed in the curve of microphones
My ears cannot hear your slander
The girl holding an instrument
It was about intimacy
a sense of belonging
change and determinacy
The identities were merging
And if my right eye were lined with many such needles
Watch out for martyrdom as self-definition
And boxes to be opened like presents
Refugee camps too dangerous to set foot in
It would never stop, even for a single moment
Always seeking various forms of utopia
They coasted in on feet
The locusts rose in a cloud
The bags were empty, a thousand or more
And were never seen again
And the streets cobbled
It's the biggest strike in history
The media are sanctioning violence

Blend III

The quickened relation of women to women   The number of trans
writers supporting her   *I might fall in love with that house*   Accents
    and the energy of those accents
Where a part of you goes   The heightening of the intonation
    on the West Bank   *Till a drizzle of tears fell on Rabi'à*
The measure of the heightening   quickness of the trigger
This is the substance of my complaint   Her bravery in showing her
    face   *Some day I will have to*
A fierceness growing out of circumstance   A pacing and an opening
Bringing friend and friend together
And so they were certain for a second
My soul, how long will you go on falling asleep
Synapses out of the body, the arm sore   The passage instantaneous
and important   *I did it by saying*   However the communication
    occurs

Blend IV

One day Rabi'à needed a piece of cloth
> You belong as much to stories as to places

So it's become a question of color, has it?
> You round the fountain with clothes on

And she threw it into the Tigris river
> A tender history missed by the foreign eye

Because I was afraid
> A half dozen faces watching

If I put both together in one hand
> Many million (twenty-three), half Syrian and Palestinian

So you call my name
> The words held in river, just letting go at the mouth

Take my prayer as it is, devil and all
> The waters rising, fear encroaching

Where can this being be found?
> It is like this, very akin, like to that

I'll open to you one spark
> You are torn, led from there, a hand in Arabic

Take my prayer, devil and all
> Poetry is not a luxury

Take my prayer as it is
> She quoted Audre Lorde

The words that mix with my prayer
>A necessity of our existence

In love, nothing exists between breast and breast
>You have to deal with people as equals

You can switch places and still belong *The one who tastes knows*

In whose presence you are blotted out
>We should all revise our clinging to borders

My tears don't stop falling
>It was this rather than that, an ear then

Nor can my burning eyes ever let me sleep
>When narratives act more efficiently than stars

Blend V

Peeling fruit in the Pharaoh's kitchen
Making an hourglass out of vulnerable bodies
Holding the curve as a place to hold to
Who cut their hands to shreds when they saw
It was in those hands, creased and held out
Delivering some lines with ears to open after
And didn't even know it
A leaf already dropping, persons, not leaves
Your house is only a stone
You could not tell from the memories not said
Where am I headed now?
The way to know, to try to listen before speaking
only a handful of dust
Autumn notes, letting go, letting be
And your house is only a stone

Note 3 on "eavesdrop": Navigating between a native and a foreign language, or more than one, and starting to do this fluidly, as you breathe in and breathe out, the more you know a foreign language, the more it becomes fluency of sorts—except it does not read fluently because it is strange and weird to have these internal mechanisms made external. These words I am using, like "internal" are finally so disappointing, which this work also attempts to enact.

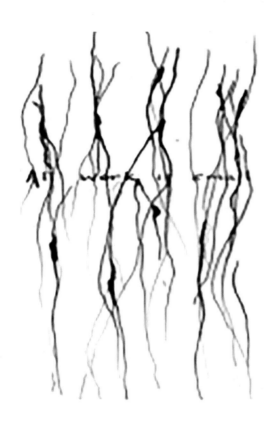

(from Rachel Levitsky, "All work is small")

EACH DIX MINUTES

Je croyais all told dans tous que tu
dee dee under which through c'est oui
for instance les parapluies here here here
évidemment so comme il devait passer son
Baccalaureate with the crowning cette
Rue these people aussitôt bien que deplorable
Élection d'où on va someone to lead non
Ce n'est pas de l'herbe the sun and the blue
Quelque chose qui ne va pas surely it's
That une tendance vers la droite and the
Straight il méritait bien plus que ça in
The drowning des couronnes like I said
Comme je t'avais dit I don't know where
I'll be in half an hour et je te parle de
la fin de l'année the end of something
oui c'est ça parmi intuitions that va-et-vient
the same colors ton pied *une* couleur mama
thank you and in that crowning elle disait
quelque chose and we together se disait
à tout à l'heure meaning much later
une fréquence seldom heard et comment
the how et respectivement a book des livres
the desire to blended into marguerite exit strategy

If in the jardin tu find it c'est
Quelque chose compared to the name
François Hollande there was a woman
Hillary Clinton les gens de pouvoir and
We haven't much la voix est séparée to
the point of no stopping here where birds
and planes mingle la voix et la machine
and something else humaine qui vide
l'humanité yet Christmas and Rosh Hashanah
revenu de plus en plus tôt. They were
to take the ferry sans but lucratif
the rain of bodies j'étais contente là
in the bubble tous qu'on a the body
l'abdomen comme deuxième cerveau
to take the knowledge back nourrir the nest
that fed you tant pis s'il n'y avait
plus the precious metals to make
ce portable na na na na riding through
la fin décidément trouble in the air
dans l'eau the crisis has arrived
tenez-vous les mains of all you hold dear on y va.

once ainsi the hats et les pieds
a ship come in voilà c'est ça to hear
but softly non non non she says
premiers mots a labyrinth of humans
rocking d'un côté à l'autre knowledge
in the machine le bateau bleu passe
gales of news encore une interruption
another explosion "ça, c'est Beyrouth" the
red wine a poison c'est toxique you
increase et toute la pizza plus more
dans l'assiette it felt good quelques moments
"you should get Instagram" pigeons even
here mon cher Lisbonne c'est vrai the flags
continuing to flap le rouge et le vert
a kind of glistening dans la porte d'entrée
a pulling at the follicles oui je peux
so in that rencontre oui we go hélas
the wishing du vent and we are not vous
n'êtes pas obligated la responsabilité n'est pas
singular let go "lâche lâche" and so

Et si tu m'avais dit all that before je ne
pourrais pas t'entendre in the music de la
quotidienne marching toward rain le savoir
ancien we are split l'expérience là
maintenant the diaper sac dropped from the
hands of the thief et Giorgio Agamben avait
tout compris except for the magic synthesizing
moments de social media à travers l'iPhone
and split second wrenched dans l'absolu
c'était ça we-in-an-interruption et nous
sommes sidérés the sand bank eloquent in
its gravity à ce moment-là the horizontal
en dehors du temps the sand keeps on
dripping le chateau detruit in a second
the paintings of Irving Petlin là et là-bas
and behind the piano les Arabes aiment les
chats thank you Liliane shokran Akram
the gay eyes de ces muscles (rappellent
Pasolini, rappellent Duras) and the director
gets all the credit et il se mettait à écrire
(Terrence Malick) là in Simone and Etel's apartment
nous avons regardé *Days of Heaven* deux
fois au Champollion and we are in love (les paysages)

Et si nous deux there in the shaft
bricoleurs of light et comment faire
there there une personne uniquement
one and the happenings *collective*
all of us se demandant après
in the water of the clouds
asking how how et elle disait
should we be en trinquant les verres
(not really asking) et à ce moment-
là it clicks into place comme dans
une photo the turmoil & bravado of
the presence Jane Wyman est aveugle
how intensity runs into religion et nous
savons tous quoi faire (we don't) mais
vous mettez la fourchette là, le couteau
là catch us licking the spoon
tellement de vélos into that zone
tout se passe walking with phones
or gestures (roues) et in that place
place et donc voilà like that continuing
ask Uljana, ask her (une pluie de langues)
decentered assuming il y avait un centre à un moment given

And how au-delà with sheets enrobés
de pensées could that entre les deux
a pocket between les dents
entre enter Colette elle-même in that
preposterous place au-desso(u)s the wink
c'était dieu in that dedans ou below
the placement of peonies la semaine des pivoines
you tie the sheets together et tu creuse
tu creuses with your children's socks
ce n'est plus en haut (extremist for
prime minister) they laugh tu creuses heaven is
in that blackness et c'est la mode
de-experienced choissisant des papiers
half the day le pétale of a poppy
regarde maman tears over a stick avalées
goûtés each emotion en produit une autre
planting tears il est temps arriving in that
split second qui est juste là maintenant now

A flash et tout ce temps-là la télévision
quelque chose d'ancien and an alarm
clock 4:37 et alors une sorte de madeleine
it was the snooze button et dans tout
cela a sleeping under the elements quatre
mains a heaving breath et tout ce temps-là
three figures une femme et deux enfants
moving within time un expérience spirituelle
presque and the slowing down si
difficile à faire in the moment so necessary
Doris Lessing disait how the breakdown
nous permet de voir yet the destruction
comme dans le divorce (each of four
hands moving orchestrée parfaitement)
necessary elle a laissé ses enfants and
to reconcile la vie et l'art to care only
about ceux qui arrivent at an equilibrium
sinon l'art it goes too far (jusqu'à la falaise)
the point being pas de sotter the words without us

Si on savait at which point the news allait
pénétrer that bit of wind et combien ça
coûtait under the arm sur les genoux
(breathing breathing) ils mentaient pour
survivre and your hands there juste là
it was cold on the hot days comment s'intégrer
tout çela the bees worked all afternoon
and morning et puis il y avait une espèce
de thin green carpet elles sont parties
never had this happened before les gens
n'arrêtaient pas de dire ça truly it
was all new c'était la même chose
no way around it il y avait quelque chose
dans son regard God has left the place
lequel? the bar, the steeple mais
de prier c'est très bien pour le corps
that's what we had heard le klaxon
des voitures the fierce buzzing all afternoons
all morning nous sommes arrivés à notre
destination except we didn't want to get off
le bus interrompu pour le match à l'Hôtel de Ville
and we on the pavements grey.

THE HANDS

M'barek Bouhchichi show "Les Mains Noires,"
curated by Omar Berrada at the Galerie Kulte in Rabat,
Morocco, spring 2016.

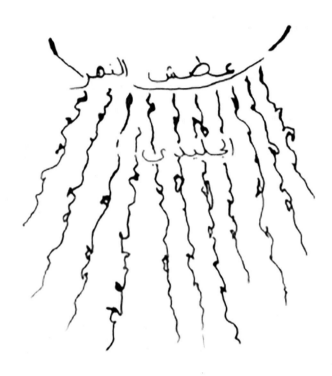

(from Cecilia Vicuña, "the glacier's thirst")

in their hands/ huge shadow/ cast by/ small grave

triangle/ darting large/ minuscule/ thin, plot

white cemeteries/ black cemeteries

in rubber/ in picture frames/ without soul

rubber debris/ left in the frame/ white above

black below/ a rapport/ other/ than service

other than/ domination/ you dig

draw/ sketch/ write/ ask them to

the hands of workers/ sculpt /hands

in those palms clenched/ something more

than sculpture/ in the crevices/ the artist's mind

joins in their hands/ countless hands/ noticed

there on the ground/ the earth held/ in the hollows

of the hands/ a rapport founded on/ the time

spent together/ a wall full/ outside/ rectangular

green/ spread like stars/ glazed emerald/ cemetery

stones/ color of the saints/ in all this white and black

because it's alive /green brings life/ given shape

on the ground/ dark meteorites/ from the sky

this blackness/ from the sky/ here on

earth/ trees upside down/ graves rooted in air

not vertical/ not horizontal/ people gripping

matter/ and in this tremendous hope/ because

emancipation/ the hands and/ the minds/ *le temps*

passé ensemble/ Tiznit / the artist participating

in a real/ time spent together hands/ minds

souls/ in this real/ the sky on the ground/ the sky on

(from a Syrian refugee, "even the stones are crying from what's
happened")

CAN WE TRANSFORM?

Rabbit tried to call the clay man back,
but when the clay man wouldn't listen,
Rabbit realized he'd made a clay man with no ears.

—Joy Harjo, *Crazy Brave, A Memoir*

Murmurations

I've seen flocks of birds switch directions
Nearly simultaneous to the micro-seconds
I've heard scientists explain it but today I'm not interested
        in scientists
Unless they can explain the human soul
How it sits and waits, waits
Hovers behind its body that is so utterly washed,
        fed, cooled and heated
How far is it from love?
Who tells us we are animals?
And reminds us what kind of animals we are
I see as many planes as birds from my skylight in Brooklyn
Are we a species meant to fly?
Things have always changed
The dinosaurs went extinct.
People built the Pyramids. Rome fell.
What has swallowed us whole?
Industrialization and tech?
The unaddressed trauma of slavery and our founding genocide?
Today I listen to an indigenous prophecy
That the female intuitive powers of the south
will rise up to meet the destructive male forces of the north

The Eagle and the Condor
I try not to be essentialist
Except that at our daughters' school

There are 20 Green Dragons taking out air conditioners, doing
       clothing swaps, making an edible garden
Mostly women from Europe
And one male director who moves as he must, with the flock
And we are birds in our hearts
Shifting directions, learning how to move together differently
That we are far from the Earth and its life and need to heal
Some women in Ecuador have formed a spirit circle
They are holding the earth sacred
I've heard many say we need to fight, how many years we have left
Ignoring the voices of all those we have trampled on to make our
       towers
I have noticed something
This is the time to transform
Individuality is overrated, lonely really
These amazing women are holding out their hands, asking us to
       stand shoulder to shoulder
And so it happens: we as a species shift directions
with the breath of our poems
we won't leave you behind

Among Brooklyn School Children

I want to give you something as
        gentle as the breeze, as strong
        as sunlight, as intricate and
        fragile as a snowflake

I want to unpave the streets for you,
        pull down the skyscrapers,
        turn the cars into horses

I want to plant old-growth trees,
        return species to
        Mannahatta, the rock spike-moss,
        whorled milkweed, elm-leaved
        goldenrod, and most of all give back
        land to the Lenape people

I want to undo that 9 of 10
        Natives of this land were killed
        by European Settlers and the slavery
        of Africans who has not been made into equality

I want Martin Luther King Jr.
        not to have been assasinated

I want us to hear the quote of King's on the school door:
        "Life's most persistent and urgent question is
        "What are you doing for others?"

I want hope, I want
     girls to be equal to boys
     and women to be equal to men

I want the reciprocity with nature
     to spread, not diminish

I want food, clothing, and shelter for all people

I want butterflies and bees,
     and the ability to imagine
     butterflies and bees

I want us to love the Earth
     as much as it has loved us so far

I want us to embrace change, even transform

I want us to remember: we have the power to love

I want us to rise up, and feel connected with all beings

I want us to think of children in Bangladesh, in Teheran,
     in Marrakech, and Tokyo, and Rio

I want us to know that we are in the richest place
     on the planet in terms of money

And that wealth comes from hundreds of years—
  the land and lives of the indigenous
  and the African Americans, and millions of immigrants
  and working-class folks

And that wealth comes from China where
  many of our clothes and plastic toys are made

And that wealth comes sometimes from
  child labor in the Congo to make our families' cell phone parts

And when we step on an airplane we are 1 out of 7 people in
  the world who have ever done so, who can afford to do so

I want us to feel the responsibility we bear for each other as joy

Because we know how to love, not only our families and friends
  and teachers

But because we have the capacity to love those we don't know

Because we have imagination—we can imagine their lives
  and what they need and love

We have the ability to feel equal to each other from the inside

And so I hand to you this cup of air for you to swallow

It belongs to you and it belongs to everyone

It will always be with you, be part of you

Your amazing magical bodies, your ability to fly like
     a bird in your mind's eye

Your ability to be in the world,
     and above all, to love,
     each other and all beings

Flying So Close to the Sun

after reading Leanne Betasamosake Simpson

My father has TIME in his hands
And we are flying to Boca Grande in a private plane
to see his oldest friend and say good-bye perhaps

Once when I wanted to meet Doris Lessing
in person, because her book *The Prisons We Choose*
to Live Inside meant so much to me

The chunnel from Paris to London was closed
because of strikes, and I had a little baby in my arms.
Doris Lessing called me to say that the weather was bad,
that I wouldn't really want to be there.

I dreamed of taking a family private plane,
with all the Moroccan family
and all the American family

With music and dancing and
togetherness, to host the one wedding
we didn't have: to be all together in the sky

To come out of our prisons simultaneously,
connected, to realize the ways we live
are constructs—that there are thousands of
ways to live

Not just marching to work on Wall Street
or marching against those who work there
though I have meditated with eighty at City Hall,

Now with the artists we forge paths,
together with everyone else, together with farmers
and teachers and lawyers and mothers

Together with anyone of any role
who can see that we need to TRANSFORM
It does not seem possible, this dream, and yet
it is all that we have

We have gone too far and none of us is pure
as I write from this plane after giving up flying
to limit fuel consumption because I know
that a simple plane flight is fatal for
        fellow souls and creatures—for us all

In the clouds I eavesdrop on the presence of ancestors
who have been especially wise. They are whispering
to us. Here, by the sun, in the earth. Why can't we hear?

How many miles have we accrued?
I recall what happens to Icarus, getting too close to the sun
in a golden chariot. Which airline does Icarus fly?

How many lives do we have, and how do we get there?
How can I tell our girls that their lives are compromised
because of ideas the patriarchy chose and still follows?

I tell my ultra-blond daughter she is half-black.
She tells me I will always be with her, that I am her only mother.
We are flying, she and I, with TIME on their side.

I too would like a divorce from billionaires but cannot have it.
Can you? I am stuck here in my beautiful life of trying to mend
a vanishing world. And so I sing to all of us.

May we hear the earth and remember the hearts of our civilizations
the women and the two spirits and all those who in their guts
embrace difference and equality and reciprocity with this planet's beings.

May our bonds be stronger than their stocks, may the freedoms
we find and create and imagine survive their power. May we RISE
together in a billion ways. All the ways are good.

May we have each others' backs. May we walk and lie down on the ground.
May we be more than do. May we be.
May we transform.

A Welcome to the Anonymous Manifesto

All of us have hearts

All of us have eyes

All of us have fingers

All of us have some connection to poetry, many of us are poets.
Some of us are artists and editors and professors and performers.
All are friends of artists and poets.

We are not equal, our traumas are not equal, some traumas are
a hundred times those next to their neighbors', yet we are all
equally animal, and we all have traumas, including the shock
of coming into the world.

And we are alive at this time.

We are in a room at this time.

We have hopes for the future.

We care about many of the people we don't know.

We care about animals and plants and trees and bodies of water.

We care about cultures we have never visited

We are in the middle of a city

Which is the financial capital

Of the earth in a civilization

That has done more damage in hundreds of years

than any other civilization

that has been and continues to be for many

an extremely popular civilization

less and less with our fascism

Nevertheless a civilization which has not been asked to apologize
and make amends

In a deep and lasting away

That has as its first value Profit and in its settler colonialist
        documents Equality and Freedom

That does what it wants to do because it is so powerful
the profit it has made on continued genocide and
enslavement and abusive labor and imprisonment and violence of
        so many

that regularly declares war at strategic times to prolong
    the imperialist patriarchy

And in this city we have tonight a space

Us, in this room, with no computers present

We have behind us and before us a history of

manifestos, especially in the last hundred years,

that matches the focus informing much of our work

a history of questioning existing structures,

of taking things apart in brilliant ways

Now I believe we have a task before us

That is stronger and more amazing than any we
Have faced as a group

Which is to go around and under and through these abuses
and buildings and corporations and technologies and intricate
oppressions which are too big and too entrenched and have
their tentacles around the world to be able to take down by force

And we must speak to the heart of things

More radically than politicians can ever do

More subtly and complexly than protest signs allow

I believe we must hold our traumas before our eyes
    As they are, micro and macro and everything in between

So that we can not run away but walk through, shoulder to
shoulder

And we must hold them with the will to live

And we must hold them with the joy of being together,
of getting to be together now

And together we can find ways to listen, and to

Create together spaces where difference and variety and
the honesty of what has been happening and what is happening
now is the value

Not just for our communities in which we actively
create and work with each other

But to reach toward and under

Where other people are valued with love, not how
much they make and what color they are, and plants and animals
are part of things, not for our benefit

91

May this manifesto in itself and the writing and teaching
go beyond the comfort of our experimental communities

Because sometimes if you take the power to say
        This is how it is, which I did as a young woman
                I am going to be a poet
        Which all have of you have done one way or another

There is so much courage in this room, much of which happens
        quietly while you are writing

Then you gather your energies, your resources, your connections
        Wrap your body and soul around it

Now I believe we need to decide collectively to be

We get to envision how we want the future to be

Not how it will be. Not that practical. Because we are poets, not
the most practical of folks usually. But how we want it to be. To inspire
others with our fierce energy for collective, diverse life

With our sense of beauty, of how communities can weave

The Racial Capitalocene is killing life on and around the Earth

And there's no machine, no political party, no individual
strong enough to undo it

It needs to be everybody who possibly can working on it
And to be people like us, who understand we are all animals
too, and there are millions of ways to live, not just being divided
by the traumas and exhaustions supremacy causes.

We need the poets to argue for the soul of life.

We are almost giving in, that this all is getting away from us.

But think, you who know this culture, this city, can you fly above
it, just you, naked in your clothes, with your pen and paper,
can you fly up above the city?

It needs to be people like us who draw and scribble how things
Can be. I think of families I have met in the Atlas mountains above
Marrakech who are depending on us to figure things out without even
knowing we exist, in countries where there are no poetry centers, where
there is a high density of poets in prison

Because if it's about following a line on your phone about koalas dying in
Australia from the fires, we will be doing this all the years to come, until
there are no phones left, just the burning and flooding.

Let's get to roots of things, because we can. And let's fly on up. Because
few among even imagine it's possible, if we take everything into
consideration, and so we don't, we don't think about it. I'm new to the
synthesis of what has been happening all this time, at a gut level, and I
have the energy now, so use my energy.

A friend I met through our late Stacy Doris told me this anecdote:

A student is trying to solve a problem and keeps coming up with different solutions, trying them, failing, trying again, casting about. The Buddha says, perhaps it is not a matter of finding the right answer, but of asking the right question.

And I believe our question is: can we **TRANSFORM** ?

Now we need to look not only to humans, who only seem to react to direct danger despite, or perhaps because, of all our intelligence, but to other species, to the murmurations of starlings by the hundreds and thousands, making intricate little changes in synchronicity with others.

Because if we believe the fire is now, we can fly, communicating in intricate peaceful ways to each other.

Let us as Poets and the friends of Poets here with us today, make a SOUND so strange and beautiful that the flocks of birds fly up, the flocks of politicians and teachers and bankers and parents and construction workers and factory workers and tech people and traffic cops.

This is our **INVITATION TO THE SPECIES.**

about the author

Sarah Riggs is a poet working on an "Invitation to the Species" in the form of a podcast/video/book with artists and intellectuals, on the relations of people to each other and the earth. This work draws on her social circles of the last seventeen years with her partner Omar Berrada between Morocco, France and the U.S, and their organization *Tamaas*, which means connection in Arabic. Its new educational U.S. branch is "Earth Arts Justice."

Eavesdrop is her 6th book of poetry in English. Her first book, *Waterwork*, was also published with Chax. *The Nerve Epistle* is forthcoming with Roof Books, 2021. As a professor she has taught at Columbia and NYU in Paris, as well as Pratt in Brooklyn in the founding years of the creative writing program. Riggs has translated 6 poetry books from French including Etel Adnan's *TIME* (Nightboat Books, 2019), which was listed for the PEN award.

Her film productions have shown at the Berlin Film Festival, the Jeu de Paume, the Tate Modern, Anthology Film Archive and other venues. Her drawings and paintings have shown at galleries internationally, and often are in conversation with her writing. Riggs' book of essays *Word Sightings* (Routledge, 2002) sketched maps for her pursuits, which seem to be about the eye and the pen, and are, it turns out, mostly about listening to others and our collective synergies on this planet.

about chax

Founded in 1984 in Tucson, Arizona, Chax has published more than 240 books in a variety of formats, including hand printed letterpress books and chapbooks, hybrid chapbooks, book arts editions, and trade paperback editions such as the book you are holding. From August 2014 until July 2018, Chax Press resided in Victoria, Texas, where it was located in the University of Houston-Victoria Center for the Arts. UHV has supported the publication of Since I Moved In, which has also received support from friends of the press. Chax is a nonprofit 501(c)(3) organization which depends on support from various government private funders, and, primarily, from individual donors and readers In July 2018 Chax Press returned to Tucson, Arizona, while maintaining an affiliation with the University of Houston-Victoria. Our current address is 1517 North Wilmot Road no. 264, Tucson, Arizona 85712-4410. You can email us at chaxpress@gmail.com.

Recent books include *The Hero* by Hélène Sanguinetti (translated by Ann Cefola), *Since I Moved In* by Trace Peterson, *For Instance* by Eli Goldblatt, *Towards a Menagerie* by David Miller, *The Long White Cloud of Unknowing* by Lisa Samuels, *Io's Song* by Murat Nemet-Nejat, and *A Day of Glass* by Steven Salmoni.

You may find CHAX at *https://chax.org/*